Your Faith
JUDAISM
By *Harriet Brundle*

PHOTO CREDITS

CONTENTS

©This edition was published in 2018.
First published in 2016.
Book Life
King's Lynn
Norfolk PE30 4LS

ISBN: 978-1-78637-025-9

Written by:
Harriet Brundle

Designed by:
Natalie Carr

A catalogue record for this book is available from the British Library.

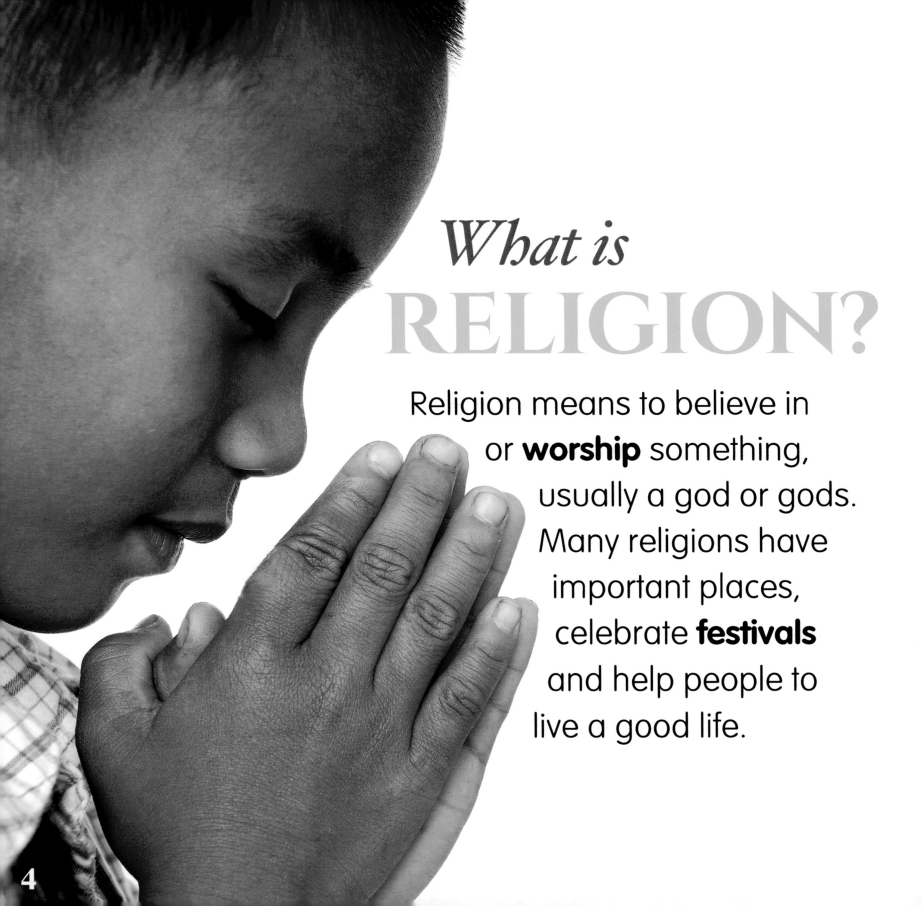

What is RELIGION?

Religion means to believe in or **worship** something, usually a god or gods. Many religions have important places, celebrate **festivals** and help people to live a good life.

There are lots of different religions. Some of the religions with the largest amount of followers are Christianity, Islam, Hinduism, Judaism, Buddhism and Sikhism.

CHRISTIANITY

ISLAM

HINDUISM

SIKHISM

JUDAISM

What Is
JUDAISM?

Judaism began over
4,000 years ago and
has millions of followers.
Jewish people follow
Judaism and they
believe in one god who
made the world.

Jewish people believe that God chose a man called Abraham and asked him to do certain tasks. Abraham did the tasks and showed others how to live their lives.

The TORAH

Hebrew Writing

The Torah is the holy book of Judaism which is printed on a scroll. It is **traditionally** written in a language called Hebrew. The Torah instructs Jewish people on how to live their lives.

The Torah must never be touched by a person's hands.

The Torah is made up of the first five books of the Hebrew Bible, which includes other important Jewish writings.

The Torah includes a list 613 mitzvot or rules. These include havingrespect for your mother and father.

PLACE *of* WORSHIP

A Jewish place of worship is called a synagogue. A synagogue is used as a place for the **community** to come together, and as a place for study.

Children are very welcome at a synagogue.

Most services are peformed in the language of Hebrew.

A person who leads a **service** at a synagogue is called a rabbi. At a Jewish service, prayers are usually sung.

Inside a SYNAGOGUE

Inside every synagogue is a special cupboard, called an Ark. This is where the Torah is kept.

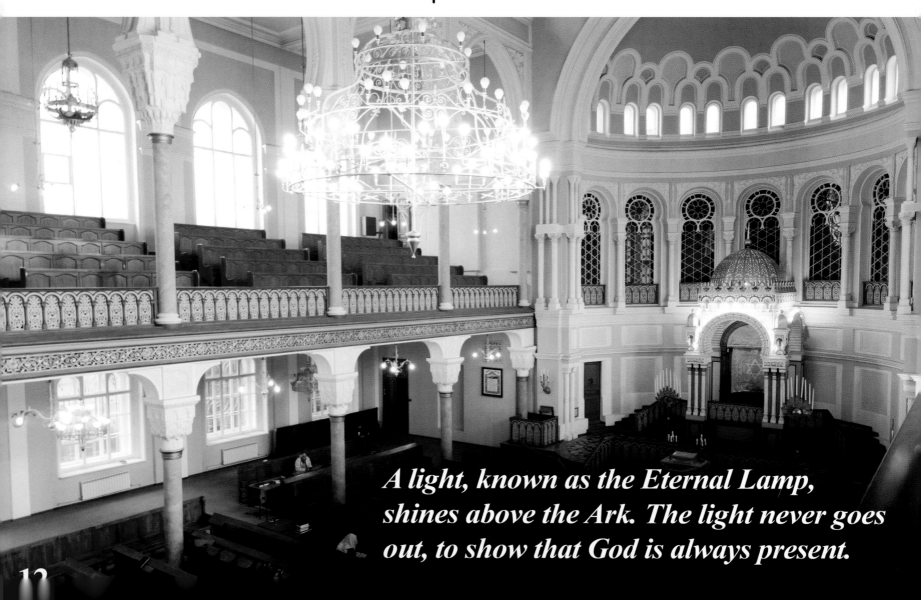

A light, known as the Eternal Lamp, shines above the Ark. The light never goes out, to show that God is always present.

Inside a synagogue, women usually wear a headscarf and men wear a special hat, called a kippah.

Kippah

Tallit

When praying, Jewish men wear a shawl called a tallit. It has lots of tassels, which represent all the different rules in the Torah.

Tassels 13

SHABBAT

Shabbat is a Jewish day of rest which happens every week. It begins at sunset on Friday and ends at the same time on Saturday. In between these times, Jewish people must not do any work.

Jewish families celebrate Shabbat by eating together, lighting candles and going to the synagogue.

*To mark the end of Shabbat there is a **ceremony** called Havdalah.*

Bat and Bar
MITZVAH

When a girl is aged 12, she becomes a bat mitzvah. When a boy is aged 13, he becomes a bar mitzvah. This means they become **responsible** for the things they do and must learn more about their faith.

A special ceremony takes place at the synagogue.
The boy or girl reads aloud from the Torah.

After the ceremony everybody celebrates together.

HANUKKAH

Hanukkah is a Jewish festival that is celebrated in the Jewish month of Kislev. Hanukkah lasts eight days.

Children will often receive a gift on each night of Hanukkah.

Hanukkah can be called the Festival of Lights, because it is celebrated by lighting candles on a menorah.

Menorah

MARRIAGE

A Jewish wedding takes place under a chuppah, which is a cloth roof held up by four poles. The couple must sign a special document, called a ketubah.

*The two people getting married usually **fast** for one day before the wedding.*

At the end of the wedding ceremony, it is tradition for the groom to stamp on a piece of glass so it breaks. This is to show that there will be both joy and sadness in life.

After the ceremony, everybody celebrates. There is usually a meal, followed by music and dancing.

Facts about JUDAISM

The most important place for Jewish people is the city of Jerusalem. Most synagogues are built with the Ark facing Jerusalem.

2 When a copy of the Torah is too worn and old to read, Jewish people bury it as a sign of respect.

3 A synagogue can also be called a shul, which means school.

4 Jewish people usually only eat kosher meat. This means the animal has been killed in a certain way.

GLOSSARY

ceremony a formal act peformed on important or religious occasions

community a group of people living in the same place

fast to stop eating or drinking

festivals times when people come together to celebrate special events or times of the year

responsible to have control of something

service a ceremony

traditionally ways of behaving that have been done over a long period of time

worship to show a feeling of respect